Rick Voyles and Carol Rice

This book is given to this Soldier by:

Jack Michelilite

in appreciation for your service.

Thank you, thank you, for all you do to keep us safe. We appreciate you!!!

High Praise for Understanding Conflict

I met Carol Rice and her husband a year ago on a flight to Atlanta. Normally, I work while flying. Fortunately, I did not. Instead, I enjoyed a detailed conversation with this very perceptive and dedicated woman whose interest in conflict resolution, empathy for others, and commitment is inspiring.

As the son, brother, and father of officers I am especially pleased to know that this book will help military families. Were I a commander deploying to or redeploying from a theater of conflict, my leadership team, chaplains, and medical professionals would be using this book to ensure that we prepare our Soldiers and their families for the stresses they will face.

I am thankful that the American people have taken an interest in our veterans and their families during this protracted war. I am especially glad that Dr. Richard Voyles and Carol Rice have produced this book that can help many to understand and cope with the stresses that result from their necessary service to our nation and others.

– Colonel Floyd J. (Jeff) Davis,
U.S. Army, Ret. –

"Conflict is misunderstood." Thus begins the book *Understanding Conflict*, and it is an undeniably powerful truth. This book is a brilliant articulation of the benefit – yes, benefit! – of addressing conflict and of the manner in which to get what you need when doing so. This book is a gift, and I recommend it to those who seek more value, more insight and even a degree of peace in their relationships and in their lives.

– Martin L. Ellin
Executive Director
Atlanta Volunteer Lawyers Foundation –

I strongly recommend *Understanding Conflict* to every military family, especially soldiers, marines, sailors and airmen deploying oversea as well as their spouses and other family members. This book is practical and in-depth explaining techniques to deal with issues encountered by the service members deployed and their families at home. Military families deal with the same issues as civilians and the additional burdens of having a critical member of the family deployed. Whether conflict in the ranks, conflict with peers or conflict at home, this book is a welcome tool that will assist every military family coping with problems that arise particular to our military. This book is a wonderful resource that may aid managing the difficulties and conflicts that CAN be anticipated or may well occur after deployment. *Understanding Conflict* provides the reader with a balanced approach to recognizing and understanding issues.

– Kim A. Fadel, President
Zephyr Solutions and Productions,
a Service-Disabled Veteran-Owned Small Business –

Understanding Conflict

A Resource for the Military Family

Published by White Feather Press.
(www.whitefeatherpress.com)

ISBN 978-0-9822487-8-2

Printed in the United States of America

Cover design created by Ron Bell of AdVision Design Group (www.advisiondesigngroup.com)

White Feather Press

Making the world a better place
One reader at a time

Table of Contents

Table of Contents (Continued)

What You Can Expect to Get Out of This Book

We will look at:

- how conflict dynamics work
- how to recognize conflict communication
- how to manage a healthy venting process using effective communication skills
- how to explore and discover the NEEDS behind your conflict
- how to get out of the PAST where people in conflict get stuck
- how to move into the FUTURE where all resolution lies
- four conflict management secrets most people don't know

Prologue

Life is hard – that's not an excuse, it isn't permission, it's just a fact. When life presents us with challenges that are outside our comfort zone, we react – and not always positively. Life in the military adds a new dimension, a new "partner" in relationships that may already be tested because of the world we live in. The economy takes its toll. There is never enough money for what we need, much less what we want. That is just plain frustrating. There is never enough time to nurture the relationships that are important to us. That can be destructive. Someone is always telling you what to do – it feels as if you have no control over your own life. In the case of the military family, this is particularly true and the end result is often conflict.

When we explore conflict in the military family, we often find that the "battle wounds" suffered are not always caused by the enemy. Our family, our friends, even we ourselves can be our own worst enemy. I liken the feeling of the Soldier who is given orders to move, to go to war, to change duty days or hours – all a source of stress on the family – to that of "caregiver burnout." It seems that you can't please everyone but you have no choice about it because you have given your word and are committed to "serve." The military family relationship is particularly vulnerable and these types of events can set off a firestorm of unexpected emotions and reactions. Because of this, it is important to understand yourself a little better in order to be able to deal with conflict constructively. Further into the book, you will find specific skills that will help you make sense of the seemingly unfair and unrealistic expectations placed on you and your family.

Conflict is misunderstood. When you think of conflict, discomfort, anxiety, pain, frustration, fear, anger, grudge, arguing, shouting, abandonment, abuse and many more negative images come to mind.

However, growth, understanding, teamwork, learning, trust, communication, cooperation, harmony, strength, friendship, unity, awareness, success, progress, insight, and increased intimacy are some of the positive things that can also result from conflict. When I present this list, almost everyone expresses surprise that intimacy is on the list. Most people do not associate intimacy increase with conflict, when in fact, you cannot have intimacy without conflict. It is no coincidence that as a conflict-avoidant culture we are intimacy starved.

Intimacy is the closeness nurtured within the gap between your differences. Without the differences, without the disagreements there can be no real intimacy. Being intimacy starved relates directly to our desire to keep conflict out of our life. Conflict is not the problem. Our lack of skill in managing conflict is the problem.

In fact, we spend more time and energy in our culture

mastering conflict-avoidance skills than nurturing the conflict management skills that will produce the positive outcomes we desire most. We are taught not to fight. We are taught to share, sacrifice, give up and give in for the greater good. This can create a calm environment – and that is good.

The problem is that often we grow up with only the skills of sharing, sacrificing, giving up and giving in as a response to conflict. We never learn skills for how to fight, when to fight and deciding what's worth fighting for. When we come across something we are not willing to give in or give up on, or share or sacrifice, we end up demonstrating our profound lack of skill. Without skills we find ourselves in the middle of a situation we are ill prepared for, totally outside our comfort zone.

While going through our daily routines, we seem to handle ourselves and our emotions well. That is because we are in what is called our "comfort zone." Within our comfort zone, we acknowledge our self-image, decide what is "familiar" and therefore comfortable, have established what we would "usually" do in a situation, rely on our habits (good or bad) and set our expectations.

Suddenly there is a change to our world as we know it:

- Orders to move to a new duty station
- Orders for an unaccompanied overseas tour
- Failed promotion attempts
- Reenlistment

- Tragedies – personal and/or professional
- Unfaithfulness – actual or fear of
- Marital disagreements – (may be related to something on this list)
- New responsibilities – (may be for aging parents that must be handled long distance, or issues with your children)

You have reached a fork in the road. You can choose a "victim" mentality or acknowledge the changes and deal with them.

What we know is that people act (or fail to act) largely to protect their comfort zone – so doing nothing is not productive. There is a payoff for choosing a "victim" mentality and not dealing with the issues. You get to stay angry, be irresponsible, have someone/something to blame for everything going wrong; have a victim identity; wallow in self-pity for sympathy, and have the illusion of power and control (when in reality you are the one allowing yourself to be controlled by the situation/person). If you choose to acknowledge the changes, then you deal with the issue that requires you to step outside of or expand your comfort zone in order to make competent and confident choices as you react.

Which method you choose depends entirely on how you handle LOSS. Loss can be disguised in so many ways – just look at the list.

- relational loss – losing a family member or friend (death/divorce/etc)
- identity loss – how you or others see you (including

your title or name)
- role loss – shift of what you do – where/how
- support system – loss of a group or community
- functional loss – such as the loss of a limb and material loss

Managing loss can help you manage conflict. The techniques you will find in this book will help you help yourself. After reading the book and going through the exercises, you will find constructive ways to talk about what's been lost and be able to express your feelings with someone you trust. More importantly, anxiety will decrease as you learn productive ways to verbalize your particular loss or losses.

If you don't address the loss, chances are, your loss will be even bigger and go in a direction that you can't control. Many people who don't address loss stay stuck in their anger, fear and/or anxiety. Then, worst of all, by ignoring or avoiding the loss/change, the problem becomes the "elephant" in the room and communication suffers a slow, excruciating deterioration. There is a marked increase in indulgence in drugs and alcohol – just short term relief. The extreme form of conflict management may even present itself in the form of suicide.

Understanding Conflict is designed to take you through the journey of loss, help you understand your response, create constructive options, make a commitment to collaborate on a plan and then execute that action plan. The exciting part of all of your hard work is that you will find ways to be more flexible, positively reinforce new behaviors and change attitudes in yourself and others. Just a heads-up for you – remember, we all work at our own pace and you may be willing to enlarge your comfort zone faster than someone else who is dealing with the same problem. It doesn't mean that they don't care or won't make a change in the way they work to resolve disputes, it just may take them more time.

There are things worth fighting for. There is a time to fight, most importantly, but there are honorable ways to fight while building personal and professional relationships.

— Carol —

On a personal note...

Our Operation: Soldier At Ease team just came back from visiting Walter Reed Hospital and had the privilege of speaking to several wounded Soldiers. They are some of the bravest people we have ever met. Behind the doors of the hospital there is so much pain, some of it is physical, much of it is emotional. As we listened to the stories of these warriors and learned what they have endured, we knew that our lives were changed forever. We talked about conflicts with parents, spouses, partners, friends, and even their care teams, that wove through the countless surgeries, therapies and treatments. For many, these personal conflicts were more painful than their battle wounds, stealing valued relationships, adding worry and fear to the healing equation. We shared our book and the conflict management secrets that can help them preserve their relationships while they establish healthy boundaries. It was encouraging to see them eagerly accept this book, knowing that each of us can make a difference as we do our part to contribute to the health and stability of our military families. Please consider sending *Understanding Conflict – A Military Family* Resource to as many Soldiers as you can today.

– Operation: Soldier At Ease Team –

Dedication

Understanding Conflict – A Resource for the Military Family is dedicated to every Service Member in every branch of the military. It is written to affirm what we all know – it takes someone special to do what you do, but that it does not come without a price. We encourage you to make a commitment to protect yourself and your family by arming yourself with the tools that will help you keep what you value most – your relationships. Thank you for making a commitment to protect us and keep us free through your service to our Nation.

CHAPTER ONE

Conflict is Misunderstood

Without conflict skills we create harm, disrespect, damage and lose valued relationships. We perpetuate the negative outcomes of conflict, reinforcing our belief that conflict is something to avoid at all cost. So we redouble our resolve, increase our conflict avoidant energies, and continue to misunderstand conflict.

> There is a seed of positive potential in all conflict.

Conflict can be positive. There is a seed of positive potential at the center of all conflict. In order to nurture this seed to flower, we must rethink our negative understanding of conflict. We must pay attention to how conflict works, and bring to conflict those skills and techniques that reinforce its positive potential. This does not mean conflict will not be hard, nor does it mean conflict will never hurt, but if it is going to be hard and hurt anyway, then why not manage it in a way that maximizes the positive outcomes we desire the most.

Let's begin by rethinking our misunderstanding of conflict by going into the personal story of a Soldier, Ken, and his spouse, Karen. They have two children, Sam and Amy, and an extended family who play a role in their everyday lives.

Ken is an ambitious young Soldier, anxious to grow professionally. He is willing to do the work and make the sacrifices necessary to make things happen. Karen is not employed. She is attending school, is a full time mother and an only child. Her parents depend on her to take care of their finances and doctors visits, etc. In exchange, they babysit for the children in the afternoons. It seems to be the perfect setting for an ideal family life, but in reality, there always seems to be a conflict about something.

—The Definition of Conflict—

A conflict results in any setting where there are incompatible goals, interests, feelings, or principles.[1] How many people does it take to have a conflict? It takes two to tango, but it only takes one to have a conflict.

---

1   Capobianco, S., Davis, M., and Kraus, L. *Conflict Dynamics Profile.* St. Petersburg, FL. : Eckard College Leadership Development Institute, 1999.

> It takes two
> to tango, but
> only one to
> have a conflict

When we think about conflict, we think of two people arguing, but we also get into conflicts with circumstances and time. Today Ken got orders to go on an unaccompanied overseas tour of duty that will include a promotion. He knows it is necessary to do the tour in order to be promoted but his wife, Karen, has just found out that she is pregnant and the baby will be born while he is gone. This job will not be open again for two years if he doesn't accept it. He and Karen are depending on his promotion to help them save money and prepare for life after the military. Ken is torn about which decision to make, and his frustration at his inability to control the timing has him very upset. All the things he needs to do at home to be "responsible" get in the way of his desire to be promoted. He is dissatisfied with his current rank, particularly when he is not moving up as quickly as he feels he could. Ken is in conflict with himself. Who will win? Giving up the tour is a solution, but it creates a whole new set of problems. They eventually decide that Ken must go. Karen moves into her roll as head of household once he leaves.

Another example to consider:

When a Soldier is deployed ,or TDY, for any length of time, it is often necessary for the spouse to take over many of the responsibilities of the partner until they can return. When Ken returned home from TDY, he and Karen argued over who should handle the checkbook. Ken had always been in charge of it prior to his deployment and Karen had been happy to let him handle it. Once he went away, Karen had to learn how to balance the checkbook, manage spending and be accountable for what money went out of the account. She found that she enjoyed the responsibility and did not want to give it back to Ken. They argued constantly about the account management and any number of things that revolved around money.

> **Incompatible feelings, principles, goals and interest can cause conflict.**

Incompatible feelings, principles, goals, interests will creep up in our personal and professional interactions, which means almost anything can cause a conflict.

—Conflict is Inevitable—

You can no more live life without conflict than you can live life without oxygen. In all likelihood you will not be able to live the rest of this week without some encounter with incompatible goals, interests, feelings or principles. Not only is it inevitable, it is essential. You cannot experience change, partnership, growth, community, learning, intimacy, effectiveness, success, improvement, insight, to name just a few without conflict.

So why is it we do not get up every morning expectant and excited about the conflict we might encounter today? Why do we not look for it, knowing it is out there, coming our way, understanding the life-giving potential it might provide today?

At a conference where I was speaking a woman blurted, "Oh, I wish you could just suck all the conflict out of my life." My immediate thought was, "Be careful what you ask for." She did not understand conflict and as a result was pleading for an outcome that most likely would create even more pain and loneliness in her life.

Conflict, at its fundamental root, is simply a request for communication: nothing more. So why are we so fearful of a request for communication? You come home from work; you ask your spouse, "How was your day?" You get no response. Adjusting your body position to maximize eye content and suggest genuine interest, you try again. "How was your day?" In reply, you get a shrug along with a soft grunt. What are the next words your spouse wants to hear out of your

> **Conflict is simply a request for communication.**

mouth?

"What's wrong, honey?"

How did your spouse communicate a desire to talk to you? By ignoring you and giving you the silent treatment. The reason I know this is a request for communication is that this delivery method works only with you in the room. Coming home one day finding the closets and drawers empty and the car gone sends the message your spouse does not want to talk to you. Getting the shrug and the grunt is really a clear offer for communication.

"I'll tell you what's wrong! Why didn't you call me?"

Strong antagonistic emotions and responses are evidence of valued issues and relationships. It takes a lot of energy to engage in a conflict. It is very hard to engage someone in an argument, or fight about something they care nothing about. Every conflict is evidence of an important issue or relationship.

Ken and Karen argued over what choice to make regarding Ken's promotion and resulting deployment. The point of the story is not who won the argument. The point is, they both valued

> **Every conflict is evidence of an important issue or relationship.**

the same thing: the security of the family. Each of them

saw a different way to ensure family security. They argued about something they cared about. They argued because they were worried about the impact of their decision on the future; which leads us to our first secret about conflict management.

Conflict Management Secret #1: People fight only about things they care about.

When someone hires me to resolve their conflict, I come knowing one thing: the people engaging in this fight care about something. One of my jobs as an effective conflict manager is to figure out what it is they both care about.

During my seminars I give out a homework assignment. Go home, find someone who says they love you and engage them in an argument. I get mixed reactions. Some laugh, saying, "That will be easy." Others, express worry. In fact, the assignment is "tongue-in-cheek," I do not really want them to start a fight. But I am trying to make a point.

Because people tend to fight about issues or relationships of value to them, my point is this: If you cannot engage them in an argument, then you have either picked an issue they care nothing about, or you are in a relationship they care nothing about.

You argue as a couple because the relationship is

important to you. All couples fight, all couples argue, because they care. When you stop caring you will stop fighting. The problem is not the fighting or arguing. The problem is, not knowing how to fight in a way that maximizes the seed of positive potential within every conflict. What if you could learn to fight (you are going to fight anyway because you care about many things) in such a way that your relationship could in fact grow as a result? Would such skill be of value to you?

> You argue as a couple because the relationship is important to you.

—The Opposite of Love —

Most people assume the opposite of love is hate. It is not. Hate is an incredibly binding emotion. If you ever get the chance to work with divorcing couples, you can see the binding power of hate. It keeps divorcing couples enmeshed.

The opposite of love is not hate; it is indifference.[2] Indifference means this person couldn't care less about either your issue or your relationship. Indifference cannot maintain the energy necessary for conflict. Think of the times you chose not to engage in a debate or conflict

---

2   The insight was introduced to me by Elie Wiesel in the video *Weapons of the Spirit*, written, produced and directed by Pierre Sauvage, 1990.

simply because is was not worth the time or the energy to you.

Here is the scary part! If we will only learn to care less about enough things, we will never be in a conflict again. In fact, no one would ever be in a conflict again if all of us would simply care less. Is that what peace looks like? It is if you define peace as the opposite of conflict. Let's not define peace that way! If conflict is inevitable, and peace is possible, then the two must be able to coexist.

> The opposite of love is not hate; it is indifference.

Conflict Management Secret #2:
You can control only two things: Yourself and your attitude.

Many of us get into a conflict when we try to control someone else's behavior, attitude, thinking, or feeling. We try to change them. When you try to control anything that is outside of your control, then you are the one out of control.

People throw out the window every morning the only two things they control. They decide to be grumpy or angry simply because it is cold or rainy outside. They let the weather decide who they are going to be today. Or they get upset and take it out on others because they got caught in traffic on the way to work. These people allow situations or circumstances to decide who they are, letting go of the only two things they have control over. The irony is, these same people then make attempts to control other people, how they act, who they are.

Effective conflict management begins with you. You control who you are and how you behave, and nothing else. Every conflict is an opportunity for you to step forward with a demonstration of who you are. When I see people behave poorly, I think, "Your skills are showing," which is to say, they are clearly demonstrating their complete lack of skills. Who will you be during your next conflict? With a little conflict understanding and a few skills *you* could be the best *you* ever, pulling out the power of the positive potential within your next conflict.

—Think About It—

Conflict is not the evil doer we think. Good, even great things, can come out of conflict. We need to take the time to understand what conflict is before we will be

> Every conflict is an opportunity for you to demonstrate who you are.

able to work with conflict, rather than working against it. When we learn to work with conflict we are better able to nurture that seed of positive potential lying dormant inside our conflicts.

Conflict is inevitable. It is impossible to live our lives without conflict. We should in fact stop trying. As simply a request for communication, we need not fear conflict. In fact, we should fear indifference. Conflict is evidence of caring.

I can control only my own actions and attitudes. When I try to control something outside of my control, then I am the one out of control.

If I am going to become an effective manager of my conflicts, then I must rethink how I look at conflict, and learn a few skills that will work to resolve the inevitable conflict coming my way. This way I afford myself every opportunity at being the best me in all of my personal and professional relationships.

> When I try to control things outside of my control, then I am the one who is out of control.

Let's get to work. Now that we have a better perspective on what conflict is, let's go ahead and begin to look at how conflict works by looking at some of the dynamics of conflict communication.

Chapter One
Understanding Conflict Worksheet

I. People fight only over things they care about.

1) Think back to the last argument you had (either at work or at home). Think about what it was you were arguing for. List below what you were valuing:

2) Think back to the last argument you had (either at work or at home). Think about what it was the other person was arguing for. List below what you think they might be valuing:

II. You can control only two things:
Your self and your attitude (who you are and how
you act).

1) Think back to the last argument you had at work.
Think about why you were arguing. List below
what you were trying to control:

2) Think back to the last argument you had at
home. Think about why you were arguing. List
below what you think they might have been valuing:

Personal Notes and Lessons Learned

Chapter Two
Conflict Communication

Communication is hard. Once we are into the conflict, communication takes on greater complication. We often see three communication dynamics occurring when people drop into conflict. Let's explore these three dynamics in order to better understand how conflict works.

Conflict Communication Dynamic #1: The Person Becomes the Problem

How does a person become the problem? Let me explain this dynamic by demonstrating how this might sound in Ken and Karen's house.

"You are not listening to me." This is a common phrase between people in conflict. I, myself, used this phrase, before I developed some conflict management skills and

techniques.

Believe it or not, this phrase can be delivered without yelling, without even a condescending tone. This phrase can be delivered simply as a matter of fact.

"You are not listening to me."

However, here is the full translation of this line, so you can understand its powerful, negative impact.

"You are not listening to me. If you were listening to me, then you would hear the clarity of my argument, feel the undeniable weight of my evidence and agree with me. You are not agreeing with me, so therefore, you must not be listening to me."

The short version is simply:

"We would not be having this argument if you were not an idiot."

There it is. The other person is the problem. Obviously, if the other person would just give in, give up and agree, the conflict would be over. But nooooo...

> We would not be having this argument if you were not an idiot!

Now Ken and Karen have to engage in the work, energy and effort to show each other how the other person is wrong. This energy is designed to change the other person: to change their thinking, feelings or behavior. Do you know how hard it is to change someone's mind, how they feel, or how they choose to act? If you have ever been in a conflict, you do.

I did not necessarily call anyone an "idiot." This was too harsh, too confrontational. To call someone an idiot makes me a mean person. Name calling might make the other person walk away, and then I would not get the chance to present my thorough explanation of why they were wrong.

Instead of name calling, Ken might say something like,

"Your conclusion does not follow your premise."

– or –

"You have not incorporated all of the relevant facts into you argument."

– or –

"You have a tendency to be judgmental... (followed with the quick jab to the heart) ...like your mother."

Even if someone had a good point, you could still make them the problem by saying something like: "Your point would be strong if you stated it this way, or in-

> **Without conflict skills, some people draw on an arsenal of verbal, emotional and psychological attacks.**

cluded this fact," so that you could undermine even good points by attacking the other person.

Without conflict skills, Ken and Karen end up drawing on an arsenal of "attack" tactics such as verbal attacks, emotional attacks, and psychological attacks. Some people even go so far as physically attacking the person they perceive as the problem in the hopes of getting them to change. Fighting, in an effort to change the other person, is a response from you making the other person the problem.

We tell people all the time, *"Violence is a conflict resolution technique. It may not always be the most effective technique, but it is still a resolution technique."* Obviously, violence is unacceptable and never recommended as a conflict management tool.

In my experience it is ineffective to tell children to never fight. This strategy teaches conflict avoidance, not conflict resolution. Instead of teaching people to never fight, I want to teach people not to make

> Teaching people to never fight promotes conflict avoidance, not conflict resolution.

the other person the problem, teaching them skills for how to get around this typical conflict communication dynamic. The way around making the other person the problem employs the technique of need exploration. By providing people with skills and techniques more effective than avoidance, we give them a choice. People will often choose the technique they believe will get them what they want.

Conflict Communication Dynamic #2: A Single Solution Mindset

Conflict is not the lack of a solution. Conflict is the result of people arguing over two different solutions. Conflict is never bereft of solutions. Most conflict managers believe conflict resolution is simply the task of finding a solution to the problem; figure out the problem and brainstorm a solution. This is unfortunately a serious problem producing myth about conflict. What is needed in a conflict is not for someone to add another solution to the list, but for parties to get beyond their single solution mindset. Consider Ken and Karen's argument below:

"You are wrong and should admit it!"

"I am not! You just don't understand me."

Can you hear the solution? Can you hear the other person as the problem?

Translation: "You cannot see the facts." (You're

the problem.) And, "You are stubborn."

Translation: "I am right." And, "You are too stupid to get me." (You're the problem.)

In the first statement the solution is: <u>Stop being stubborn</u>. In the second statement the solution is: <u>Understand me</u>.

Nobody comes to a conflict without a solution in mind. Conflict exists because each has a solution the other cannot accept. They are in conflict over differing solutions. Each person believes they have a clear understanding of the situation and based upon their evaluation know exactly what would balance the scales of justice.

Ken and Karen are stuck on their solution. It is what we call in conflict management: their "position." It is hard for people to give up their position. Giving up their position suggests that the other person's position is right. To agree with the other person's solution suggests that your position is wrong. People do not like to be wrong, "I may not be right, but I know I am not wrong."

A single solution mindset is one of the things that get individuals stuck when entering into a conflict. The way around a single solution mindset employs the tech-

> Overcome a single-solution mindset using need-exploration techniques.

nique of need exploration.

Both Ken and Karen are very, very good at coming up with solutions, quick to describe a cause and to outline a remedy for the conflict. It is not solutions that resolve conflicts; it is need exploration and negotiation that resolve conflicts. We are great problem solvers, but lousy need explorers. When great problem solvers approach a conflict without doing need exploration they often create more problems than the one they started with. Even good solutions without adequate and clear need exploration can be dissatisfying at best and insulting at worst.

We will get to the skill of need exploration in Chapter four. We will need to spend a lot of time there in order to communicate the importance of this often overlooked skill in conflict management.

But before we go there, let's talk about the third conflict communication dynamic.

Conflict Communication Dynamic #3: An Imbalanced Personal State

We all live within a balanced personal state between our emotions and our intellect. Each is a source of data within our decision making process. When we get into

> We all live within a balanced personal state between our emotions and our intellect.

conflict, we tend to silence one of these data sources and begin operating out of an imbalanced personal state.

I don't know who you are, which voice you silence within yourself, but I have a tendency to push out and silence my emotional voice, overcompensating with my intellect. Anyone shocked? I didn't think so.

When you silence your emotional side you look and sound calm, cool and collected in the midst of the conflict. Looking at you and listening to you, one would not necessarily believe you were even in a conflict, because your behavior does not fit the stereotype of what a conflict looks like: shouting or strong emotional outbursts.

However, by cutting off your emotional side, you become numb to the nature of your connection with the other person in the conflict. Some become cold and calculating, bent on revenge. They end up measuring the amount of the other person's suffering that is necessary for them to feel better about what they perceived was done to them. While they look and sound reasonable, in reality, inside, they are plotting your pain. They hurt and want you to hurt as much, if not more, than they are hurting. Only then will there be any rebalancing

> By cutting off my emotional side I become numb to the nature of my connection with the other person.

the scales of justice.

When Ken and Karen are fighting like this, it severs the connection between them. They will seek retribution at the expense of their relationship. The problem that is created when they do this is, that when they feel better, when they are back in a balanced personal state, when the emotional voice is allowed back into awareness, they want the connection to continue. They want the relationship to have then been repaired after each has suffered the other person's retaliation. Guess what. This response does not work and results in damaging relationships.

The logic is faulty (as it always is when the intellect tyrannically suppresses the emotion's voice). The logic follows an authoritarian model of punishment and reward exemplified by the saying: "The beatings will continue, until morale improves!" People wrongly worked out of the premise that, if you suffer every time you hurt me then, like Pavlov's dog, you will make sure to never hurt me again in order not to suffer a more severe shock for your behavior. Of course this strategy fails. It is wrong on so many different levels, not the least of which it is an abuse of power and a serious boundary violation.

The other option available, when operating from an imbalanced personal state, is to suppress and silence the intellect, letting the emotional voice rule the day. This is often the stereotype we have of people in conflict. We picture people screaming and yelling at the top of their lungs, maybe throwing things or throwing themselves around the room. It seems every text book on conflict management admonishes people not to become emotional during conflict, that emotions are the catalyst for escalating conflict.

"Don't be so emotional."

"When you calm down and become reasonable, then we can continue this conversation."

The admonition implies, and almost stresses, turning off the emotions is a necessary component to successful conflict resolution. While this is somewhat true, it masks the danger of the tyranny of the intellect and reason.

The problem is not our emotions. The problem is our imbalance. The result I often see is the over-rational person criticizing the over-emotional person for being "emotional." Both are in an imbalanced personal state and a terrible position to effectively resolve this conflict.

A solution offered out of an imbalanced personal state is in danger of generating resentment, distrust, manipulation, misuse of power and boundary violations. I do not want Ken and Karen making decisions from within an imbalanced personal state.

> The problem is not our emotions. The problem is our imbalance.

We tend to gender stereotype this imbalance, seeing women as typically silencing the intellect and becoming emotional, seeing men as typically silencing the emotions and becoming very intellectual. While men have been rewarded more often in our culture for maintaining an imbalanced personal state, it is a bad assumption to go into a conflict expecting this stereotype. There are as many women capable of being cold, calculating, bent on revenge, as well as many men who become emotionally driven during a conflict.

> **Both intellect and emotion are necessary to a healthy conflict resolution.**

I cannot tell you the number of women in our seminars who have found hope and affirmation from this concept of imbalance. Because of the stereotype, women often feel the brunt of the western bias for reason and intellect. They tell stories of feeling they have to go along with the oppression of emotionality. They have been expected to participate in a resolution process they feel is one sided and wrong.

"You mean emotions are not a bad thing?" Yes! Emotions are not a bad thing. Emotions, even passionate, loud, intense emotions are not bad, and there are appropriate and inappropriate ways to communicate our emotions, even our intense, passionate, loud emotions. Emotion out of balance with the intellect is a bad thing.

Intellect out of balance with the emotions is equally bad. Both are necessary for a healthy decision making process, and therefore, both are necessary for an effective resolution process.

— Getting Back the Balance —

If you rush the conflict management process, you risk people making decisions in an imbalanced personal state. Then, when they calm down, get back into balance, begin seeing more clearly, they often resent and regret the decisions that were made. The result is suspicion of the process used to resolve the conflict, as well as resentment for the outcome.

> A healthy venting process allows me to restore connection to myself.

There are two techniques when addressing this conflict communication dynamic. The first technique is managing and maintaining a healthy venting process. The second technique is need exploration. These two can be effectively combined, but to promote a better understanding, we will separate these two techniques here, looking at the venting process in Chapter 3 and addressing the technique of need exploration in Chapter 4.

A healthy venting process allows Ken and Karen to "let off steam" that builds up inside, silencing one of the two voices necessary for healthy decision making. Think of a balloon. Inside the middle of this balloon is a flexible partition. Above the partition represents your emotional voice. Below the partition represents your intellectual voice. As long as the partition is in the middle you have balance and two healthy voices informing your decision making. During conflict, pressure builds on one side or the other, depending upon who you are. As this pressure builds, the partition moves in the opposite direction, squeezing the space of one voice into a smaller and smaller portion, causing that voice to become weaker and quieter.

A healthy venting process is a connection restoration process. It allows them to restore connection to themselves, restoring balance between emotions and intellect. The pressure is removed and the connection (with self balance) and the one they are in conflict with is restored. In some cases, their connections can even intensify.

Venting will take two characteristically different forms. One will be what we stereotypically expect: emotional outburst. The other: over intellectualizing. Either way, healthy venting is often necessary to allow a person to retrieve personal balance.

To allow someone to vent on you during a conflict is a masterful skill. It is not easy. We have to distinguish between healthy venting and verbal abuse, between healthy venting and boundary violation. I am not asking you to lie down and take it. I am asking you to employ the techniques of a skilled conflict manager in order to take this conflict in the direction of resolution. The techniques associated with healthy venting management are predominantly communication skills. Your goal will be to keep the door of communication open.

We will show you five communication techniques for keeping that communication door open in Chapter 3.

Chapter Two
Conflict Communication Worksheet

I. The Person is the Problem
"You are not listening."

A great way to identify ways you make the other person the problem is to review the list of statements you made when venting on a friend about the person you are in a conflict with.

"She doesn't care about me."

"He never listens."

"He is lazy."

"He cares more about the military, than he does me."

"She is controlling."

"She suffocates me."

"My boss is a control freak."

"He doesn't carry his weight around here."

"She doesn't carry her weight around here."

"He wants to go overseas and leave me with all of the family problems."

Think back to your last argument. Write comments you made or thought of making that casts the other person as the problem.

II. Single Solution Mindset

"You are wrong and should admit it!"

"I am not! You just don't understand me."

Can you hear the solution? Can you hear the other person as the problem?

> *Translation: "You cannot see the facts." (You're the problem.) And, "You are stubborn."*
>
> *Solution: Stop being stubborn.*

> *Translation: "I am right." And, "You are too stupid to get me." (You're the problem.)*
>
> *Solution: Understand me.*

Take the statements below and identify the solution:

1) "She doesn't care about me."

    Solution_____

2) "He never listens."

    Solution _____

3) "He is lazy."

    Solution _____

4) "He cares more about the military, than he does me."

    Solution _____

5) "She is controlling."

    Solution _____

6) "She suffocates me."

    Solution _____

7) "My boss is a control freak."

    Solution _____

8) "He doesn't carry his weight around here."

    Solution _____

9) "She doesn't carry her weight around here."

Solution _____

10) "He wants to go overseas and leave me with all of the family problems."

Solution _____

III. Healthy Venting

1) Here are some ways to manage healthy venting:

- Walk the dog
- Watch TV
- Go to a movie
- Sing
- Go to a coffee shop
- Vent to a friend, asking them just to listen (and not take too much stock in what I say)
- Write a letter (then destroy the letter without sending it)
- Go to the gym

2) What are some of the ways that work for you when managing your own healthy venting?

3) It takes me, on average, about 2 hours to "simmer down," restore my connection with myself (balance). About how long does it take you? Write a number then circle a measure of time:

_____hours/days/months/years

*If you have a difficult time answering this question, measure the amount of time between your argument and your apology (or feelings of regret, or feelings that you might have gone too far).

**Another way is to measure how long it takes for you to miss the connection you had with the other person before the argument began (you want things back the way they were before the conflict).

Personal Notes and Lessons Learned

CHAPTER THREE
Developing Communication Skills

Communication skills do not resolve conflicts. It is the purpose of good communication skills to create clarity: both rational clarity and emotional clarity. The purpose of communication skills in conflict management is to keep the door of communication open.

The reason good communication skills are so important to Ken and Karen, when they are in conflict management, is that you cannot resolve a conflict with someone you are not talking to. Communication skills, then, play an important role in conflict management, but they will need more skills to get them to resolution. In fact, there are three distinct skill sets necessary to be an expert conflict manager: communication skills, resolution skills and negotiation skills. Communication skills are not enough.

Some conflict management books suggest reflective listening as the skill necessary for resolving conflicts. One author proposed that reflecting back what was said by the angry, or disagreeable person, would eventually target what needed to be done to make the situation better and end the conflict. To believe clarity resolves conflict, you must assume that lack of clarity is the cause of conflict. However, in the midst of incompatible goals, interests, feelings, or principles, clarity that our goals are incompatible does nothing to resolve the incompatibility.

> Keeping communication open is important when managing a healthy venting process.

Reflective listening is an excellent communication skill, but it is not enough to resolve conflicts. "I statements" is another excellent clarity skill, but will only take you so far when trying to deal with conflict.

Keeping the door of communication open is probably most important when managing a healthy venting process. Often in a conflict you may find yourself having to do both: keep communication open, and manage a healthy venting process. I have found communication skills to be the best way to navigate through a healthy venting process and set the scene for using resolution and negotiation skills.

But be careful. There is a big difference between effective venting management and resolving a conflict. Codependency in conflict can allow venting to be a crutch. Do not think that because venting has been successful the conflict is over. Don't even be seduced into thinking that it is almost over. Calm people, with great communication skills do not a conflict resolve. Remember, communication skills are designed only to keep the door of communication open. Your resolution skills will get you across that threshold.

Here are five techniques you can use to keep the communication door open and move people toward resolution.

- Summarizing and Paraphrasing
- Asking Probing Questions
- Identifying and Naming Emotions
- Validating Whenever Possible
- Finding the Positive Request

The first four are fairly familiar, so I will offer brief descriptions. In my experience, the fifth one is a little known but powerful technique, so I will spend more time with "Finding the Positive Request." If you will master this one, it will change all of your conflict communication for the better.

— Summarizing and Paraphrasing —

Summarizing and paraphrasing are good techniques for keeping the door of communication open. When summarizing you repeat back the other person's statement using their key words. When paraphrasing you want to pull out some of the toxic language while keeping the substance of the other person's statement or comment.

Conflict often shows up as impatience. When a Soldier comes home, he/she has an idea of when a meal should be served. "Dinner is at 1800." While overseas, dinner was always ready at 1800, no matter what else was going on. 1800 comes and no dinner. Ken is upset that there is no dinner and demands to know why it isn't ready as he stands at the door watching his wife and child work on a school project that is due the next day. To Karen, it is perfectly clear that something else has priority over the meal and she will serve it (or they will go out) when she has finished what she is doing.

> Ken: "I don't understand why there is no dinner on the table. Dinner is supposed to be ready at 1800 every day. You know that is when I expect to sit down to eat."

A summary would look like this:

> Karen: "So you would like for me to stop whatever I am doing and make sure that your dinner is on the table at 1800 each day."

There isn't really much toxic language here, so let's make the conversation worse:

> Ken: "You are so lazy. You are supposed to cook my dinner and have it on the table at 1800 every night. That's your job, to take care

of my needs. You are not doing a good job. You should be more thoughtful and considerate of me."

Karen: "So you would like for me to have your dinner on the table at 1800 every night from now on."

Notice that summary and paraphrase does not imply agreement or guilt. By using this technique I keep the other person talking, thereby keeping communication open.

—Asking Probing Questions —

Asking probing questions is a great door propping technique and critically important when managing a healthy venting process. The goal and tone for these questions is to be exploratory. Ken and Karen should be trying to find out how the other person is seeing the situation, and how they are coming to the conclusions they are presenting. In short, each is trying to understand the thinking process.

> You cannot defend yourself and seek to understand the other person at the same time.

WARNING: there is usually someone in the room who wants to understand the other person's thinking process in order to find the flaws in their thinking, do them the favor of pointing this out, and correcting this for them. This feeds the conflict and the venting. Don't do this. Are you willing to listen when someone says that you might not be seeing the situation clearly?

To ask in order to correct makes you defensive. You cannot defend yourself and really seek to understand the other person at the same time. Asking in order to correct will often slam the door of communication shut. As soon as you try and correct their understanding, you poorly begin the resolution part of the conflict resolution process. You correct them assuming,

> *"If you had the correct understanding of this situation, then we would not be having this conflict. A correct understanding, which I just happen to have, will resolve this conflict. Listen and I will explain to you where your misunderstanding lies."*

Also please note this is a classic, "the person is the problem" statement.

Correcting their understanding of the situation is not a useful resolution technique. Besides, this is not the resolution stage of the conflict. This is the venting

> **Keep them talking by asking probing questions.**

stage. The danger of communication breaking down is very likely. You need to use a technique that will increase the chance of continuing this conversation so you can get to the resolution stage. Keep them talking by asking probing questions.

Think of yourself as an explorer in a strange and wondrous landscape. You are trying to learn your way around this new terrain. You are asking in order to understand them, not in order to fix or correct them.

Remember the argument potential over a delayed dinner? (Karen is helping their son Sam with a project that is due the next day.) Some probing questions I might ask Ken are:

> *"Hmmm. You seem very concerned about having dinner tonight at 1800. Why is that?"*

Or, I could ask,

> *"Why are you worried about whether or not we will have dinner right at 1800 tonight?"*

For those of you more direct and to the point, this wording will work just fine. I like to soften it just a bit in order to minimize the chance of a defensive response. Some other examples could be:

> *"Would you like to help Sam with the project so that I can stop and get dinner ready?"*

> *"Would you like to make your special chili tonight while I help Sam finish his project?"*

> *"I was planning on ordering dinner in – in*

fact, the pizza is on its way and should be delivered any minute."

"It sounds like you are really hungry. Why? Did you not have a chance to eat lunch today?"

Of course the smart mouth in me wants to say:

"Why is it my job to get dinner on the table every night? I work too!"

"If you want dinner, go cook it yourself!"

"I'm sorry, the chef quit today and I haven't hired a new one yet!"

When asking probing questions, one question leads to another, and to another until the other person has a chance to tell you soooo much about themselves. People are often very willing to talk about themselves. After all you are asking them questions about a subject they are expert on: themselves. Ken and Karen can use this to their conflict management advantage.

However, each must be continually aware of tone and timing. Their tone needs to sound like genuine curiosity, inquisitive, exploratory. Your timing must not sound interrogative, rapid-fire, badgering.

— Identifying and Naming Emotions —

The ability to identify and name emotions at this stage of the conflict helps me keep doors open and helps me to manage a healthy venting process. To help identify Karen's emotions, I could ask:

> *"You seem very upset about something I said or did. Can you tell me what happened?"*

> *– or –*

> *"I can see you're frustrated. Can you tell me why?"*

Identifying my own emotions can also keep conversation going.

> *"I can see you are upset with me. I feel a little defensive and unappreciated. It would help me if you could explain what I did to upset you."*

IMPORTANT NOTE: Please understand, in no way should you stand there and take whatever verbal abuse the other person feels the need to spew out. This is simply a description of a healthy venting process. It suggests you may be in the presence of loud, even antago-

> **If you have to leave to protect yourself and your boundaries, then do so.**

nistic emotions. These skills can get you through this and into the resolution phase of the conflict. Use your communication skills to keep the door open, manage venting in productive, healthy ways, and set yourself up for the resolution stage of the conflict when you can and for as long as you can.

I am trying to describe how to manage a <u>healthy</u> venting process. When someone confronts you with verbal abuse (any abuse really), they are practicing boundary abuse which is neither healthy for you nor for them. If leaving the conversation means protecting your self and your boundaries from abuse, then leave and regroup later, if you can.

— Emotions and Anger —

Let's talk for a moment about one emotion that is no stranger to conflict communication: anger. Anger begets anger. It is part of the natural process of anger. There is nothing wrong with anger, it is just a feeling; it is not a bad thing. So relax a bit.

Anger is our body's natural warning system of impending danger. When someone angry confronts you, even if they are not yelling, even if they are managing their anger in appropriate ways, your body will respond with anger. An angry person, approaching you, standing in front of you, within your general proximity is, as far as your body is concerned, impending danger. It is not your body's job to evaluate their threat level, the seriousness or intensity of their anger, or to evaluate any likelihood that their anger might produce physical harm your body's job is simply to warn you. It is your job to process the feeling.

The textbooks describe this as escalating conflict. But, in fact, what is happening is not escalating conflict. It is your body picking up on the other person's anger. Escalation will occur every time two people with poor or negligible conflict skills, unable to process (not suppress) their emotions engage in a conflict. What the books are describing are two skill- less people in an imbalanced personal state. To describe this as the natural dynamics of conflict is like video taping a seven year old swinging a baseball bat and describing, in detail, this swing as an example of how bats are swung.

> Listen to your feelings. Learn what they are trying to tell you.

Listen to your feelings. Your emotions are a valuable source of information in any situation, not the least of which is in a conflict situation. Your body knows things your mind does not know. Listen to your feelings. Learn what they are trying to tell you. Use the information to identify which conflict management techniques and tools to utilize.

There are inappropriate and unhelpful ways to express your anger. In conflict, emotions are a problem only when they overpower and silence the intellect (remember

> Anger is only a problem when we behave inappropriately.

Imbalanced Personal State in Chapter Two?). Anger is a problem only when, instead of listening to and hearing this emotion, we act out and behave inappropriately. Anger itself is not the problem. It's the permission we give ourselves to misbehave when we feel anger that needs to change, not our feelings. The mantra should be "feel the anger and stop the inappropriate behavior," not "stop the anger."

Neither anger nor emotions are the problem. So what do we do with emotional outbursts and anger as natural characters in a conflict? Expect them to show up and don't allow them to distract you from your role managing the conflict. It is the purpose of communication skills to create clear communication: both rationally clear and emotionally clear. If you need further work in this area, find a good therapist to help you.

— Validating Whenever Possible —

In your conflict communication, validate whenever you can. This is another way to keep your communication open. Think back to the dinner argument. Karen could validate Ken by saying something like:

> *"I really appreciate you saying something to me about this. Even though you are upset, I am*

glad you had the courage to speak directly to me about your concern."

After all, Karen could simply walk away or throw Ken's dinner in his face. Or, she could validate his perspective with something like:

"Wow, the way you describe it, I would be upset too."

Note that in stating it this way, she is not agreeing with Ken's assessment of the situation. She can validate without necessarily agreeing.

I was in a committee meeting once, where during the conversation one of the committee members got so mad at me, he got up from the

> Validate a healthy venting process and a healthy response to anger.

table and left. You could feel the tension in the room. The rest of us continued the conversation. A few minutes later he returned to the meeting and to the conversation. At the end of the meeting, I turned to him and thanked him for caring enough about our relationship to leave the room rather than "attack" me.

I validated his healthy venting process, his healthy response to his anger. We still work together on some things and we still do not always see eye-to-eye on issues.

Consider using some of these statements for validation:

"You are right on that point."

"I agree with you there."

"I couldn't agree more."

"We agree on the issues, but we see them quite differently."

"I can see how you might see that working."

Remember, this is not a technique designed to set anyone up or to offer a back handed compliment. Validate, whenever you can; emphasis on 'whenever.'

In some conflict management circles, we refer to this as the "thank you" technique.

"I want to thank you for coming to me."

"I want to thank you for your honesty."

"I want to thank you for the respectful way you are handling this situation."

"I want to thank you for not being passive aggressive."

"I want to thank you for valuing our relationship."

Validation can be a moment of shock and surprise to the angry or emotional person. They are expecting a fight. In fact, they came in prepared for one. They practiced all last night, reviewing in their head, powerful come-backs. (Don't tell me you never did this).

Agreement or validation on a point is not what they expect. It throws their "script" off and they have to regroup, and often rethink a response to unexpected validation. It is this momentary opening where communication has a chance to grow into conversation, moving from debate, to discussion, and on to dialogue.

> Inside every criticism is a positive request.

— Finding the Positive Request —

This last technique, Finding the Positive Request, is harder to learn. Once you learn it, it is easy to use. Of the five techniques this is the one to use the most. Right now, let's see if I can explain and demonstrate it in a way you will be able to grasp and practice it.

Inside every single criticism is a positive request. It doesn't matter what the criticism is, a positive request lies within it. The beauty is: most criticism comes within the context of conflict. Your job, then, as a manager of conflict, is to find the positive request.

The positive request is not, I repeat, not, putting a positive spin on the criticism. The other day we were at lunch when the cashier made a comment criticizing the gas shortage in our area. Another customer did not miss a beat, "Yes, but the traffic is so much better now." This is an example of putting a positive spin on a criticism. This is NOT the technique being taught here.

The positive request technique is a <u>translation</u> skill, not a <u>point of view</u> skill. You will need to learn to translate "criticism language" into "positive request language." Let's start with a simple example.

In most training seminars, someone in the room will say: "Man is it cold in here!" This is a criticism of the room temperature. We all know the positive request translation. "Would you please turn the heat up?"

This is a translation skill. Like any translation, accuracy may require the use of more words than the number of words used in the original language. Your goal is to translate the criticism into "positive request language" using as many words as necessary to capture the request within the "criticism language". Like any mastery of another language, perfecting this skill takes practice.

This technique works with any criticism.

> *"You are the worst leader we have ever had."*

> *"You never listen."*

> *"You are a miserable and worthless human being."*

> *"This project is a complete waste of time."*

> *"Life stinks."*

Your job is to find the positive request.

> *"So, you would like to have a better leader."*

"You would like to be with someone who listens more."

"So, you would enjoy being around happy human beings."

"You like to work on important projects."

"You wish life was better."

There are three things to note about this technique: 1) if you get it wrong, communication continues; 2) when done well, the focus of the conversation shifts to where it needs to be; and 3) the temptation to slide immediately into resolution is dangerously strong.

1) Getting it Wrong

Remember, the goal is to keep the door of communication open. If your translation attempt is a dismal failure and the other person corrects you, then communication continues.

Criticism: "This conversation is a complete waste of time."

First translation attempt: "You only like to talk about what you want to."

Correction: "No. It is not that it has to be what I want to talk about. It's just that I don't think this subject is going to provide the resolution we need."

Notice that communication continued. The door is open to follow up with a probing question. Try saying something like:

"So, what do you think would work better?"

Though your translation is wrong, you still accomplish your goal. The person in conflict with you usually will not hesitate to correct you. The door is still open.

2) Doing it Well

When done well, the focus of the conversation shifts to the only two things the criticizing person can control.

Criticism: "You never listen."

Translation attempt: "So, you would like to be with someone who listens more."

Critic's response: "Yes. That is what I want."

Notice that the criticism, "You never listen" focuses on you. You are the recipient of the criticism, the subject of the sentence. The person in conflict with you is pointing an imaginary finger in your face. The shift comes in the translation. "So, you would like to be with someone who listens more." Here it comes, "Yes. That is what I want." Who are they talking about now? In the third line, the critic is the subject of the sentence. The critic is now talking about themselves instead of you. See, the only thing they have control over is themselves.

— The Number One Mistake Novices Make —

Summarizing instead of translating is the number one mistake novices make when practicing this technique.

Criticism: "You never listen."

Translation attempt: "So, you don't think I listen well."

Critic's response: "I know you don't listen well."

This translation attempt is a summary, not a translation. In the first line, the criticism points an imaginary finger in your face. The second line, because it is a summary of the criticism also focuses on you. "So, you don't think I listen." Therefore the third line becomes further criticism of you. Notice that the shift to the critic does not take place when you summarize.

Let's do them all:

Criticism: "You are the worst leader we have ever had."

"So you don't think I am a good leader," is a summary.

"So, you would like to have a better leader," is a translation.

Criticism: "You never listen."

"So, you don't think I listen well," is a summary.

"You would like to be with someone who listens more," is a translation.

Criticism: "You are a miserable and worthless human being."

"You think I am a miserable, worthless human

being," is a summary.

"So, you would enjoy being around happy human beings," is a translation.

Criticism: "This project is a complete waste of time."

"You hate this project," is a summary.

"You like to work on important projects," is a translation.

Criticism: "Life stinks."

"You hate your life," is a summary.

"You wish life was better," is a translation.

If you compare the difference, one thing you will note is the absence of the "I" in the translation. Another thing you might notice in the last two examples is that while the summary sounds a lot like the translation, the summary is still negative. Remember, you are looking to uncover the positive request. Practice this technique and work on staying away from summarizing.

3) Temptation

The third thing to be aware of is the natural, powerful temptation to slide immediately into problem solving and solution suggesting.

Criticism: "You never listen."

Translation: "You would like to be with someone who listens more."

Response: "Yes, I would."

Temptation: "Ok. I'll listen. What do you want to say?"

I cannot warn you enough of the overwhelming power of this temptation in our culture. We all seem to be excellent problem solvers and solution suggesters, but this is not what resolving this conflict requires right now. Giving into this temptation and suggesting a solution at this point only indicates how little you understand how conflict works. Yet this is a mistake almost everybody ends up making.

> **Do not slide immediately into problem solving and solution suggesting. Resist the urge!**

Using the temptation phrase will keep the door of communication open and in that regard it is an excellent comment. However, if you believe you have resolved this conflict by offering to listen, then you will be mistaken and in for an uncomfortable surprise. What is causing this conflict is not the fact that you do not listen, but the fact that the person confronting you does not feel heard; two very different things. So, will listening to them make them feel heard? Maybe, but probably not. Why are they not feeling heard? What would have to happen for this person to feel heard? What were the circumstances in the past when they felt heard? These are **Need Exploration** questions.

At the end of the communication stage and the beginning of the resolution stage of this conflict is need exploration. Do not use Finding the Positive Request as your segue into solving the problem. Use it to launch Need Exploration. The most important and least known resolution skill is Need Exploration. Let's look at how it is done and what it means to managing conflicts.

Chapter Three
Communication Skills Worksheet

Positive request exercise:

1) List as many criticisms as you can think of below:

2) Translate the criticisms list above into positive requests:

3) Identify the translation attempts below with either an 'S' for summary, or with a 'T' for translation:

Criticism: "You are a moron."

a. _____Translation attempt: "So, you think you are smarter than me."

Criticism: "I can't stand whiny people."

b. _____ Translation attempt: "You want to be around up-beat people."

Criticism: "This book is stupid."

c. _____ Translation attempt: "You don't think this book is worth reading."

Criticism: "Tomorrow is going to be a bad day."

d. _____ Translation attempt: "You would rather tomorrow not come."

Criticism: "All politicians lie."

e. _____ Translation attempt: "You believe politicians cannot tell the truth."

Criticism: "I don't like you."

f. _____ Translation attempt: "You wish I would leave."

4) Take the summaries in exercise number three

and turn them into translations:

a. Translation:

b. Translation:

c. Translation:

d. Translation:

e. Translation:

f. Translation:

Personal Notes and Lessons Learned

CHAPTER FOUR

Exploring Needs

We are great problem solvers. We are lousy need explorers. I will demonstrate this with a true story I adapted from Fisher and Ury's book *Getting to Yes* [1] about two kids arguing over an orange.

You have two kids, one orange: conflict. What do you do? In every training seminar the group always solves this problem in a second or less. "Cut the orange in half." Problem solved. Conflict ended. Get back to whatever important thing you were doing.

The danger here; the danger every time you problem solve, is you solve a problem that does not exist. I see it happen so often that I have taken to distinguishing be-

---

[1] Fisher, R.,Ury, W., & Patton, B. (1991). "*Getting to Yes: Negotiating agreement without giving in*" (2nd ed.) New York: Penguin

tween a solution and a resolution when I teach.

Two things happen when you solve problems that do not exist. First the conflict does not go away. It goes underground to surface later. And second, the people you have "helped" end up resenting you, the problem solver, for both your resolution process and its outcome.

Ken and Karen's children are arguing over the orange. By focusing on the orange, it appears Karen has suggested solving this problem by splitting the orange so they both get part of it. However, ultimately the problem was not having only one orange. The problem was why the children needed the orange. Lets look at their behavior when she gave them each their half of the orange.

> Do not solve a nonexistent problem. Instead, find the underlying need.

Amy took the orange, peeled it and ate the inside of the orange. Sam took the orange, peeled it, threw the inside away and used the peel for a science project.

What every problem solver assumes is the children want to eat the orange. Every problem solver in that room ends up solving a problem that does not exist. Instead of solving Sam and Amy's problem, let's explore their needs.

What is the need of Amy who ate the inside of the orange? The need is not the orange, it is hunger. How many different ways are there to meet her hunger need without the orange? There are many, many options available:

> *"Honey, I just baked a chocolate cake. It's in the kitchen, so help yourself."*

> *– or –*

> *"Honey, you can have anything you can find in the refrigerator."*

But what if Amy's need is nutritional? She still has many ways available to meet that need. The chocolate cake is not one of them. This leads us to a third secret about managing conflict.

Conflict Management Secret #3: There is ALWAYS more than one way to meet a need.

Resolution skills resolve conflicts, because there is always more than one way to meet a need. You exponentially increase the chance of finding a resolution by creating multiple options that will meet their need.

What is the need of Sam who threw away the inside of the orange? The need could be succeeding in the science project; it could be getting a good grade; it could be not failing the class; it could be getting into a well known science program or scholarship; it could be impressing a girl in class or on the project.

> **Resolve conflict by meeting the person's need.**

Whatever the need, and only Sam will be able to tell you, there are ways to meet any of the above needs that do not necessarily employ the single orange they are fighting over.

Everybody comes to the conflict with an "orange." It is their single solution (remember Single Solution Mindset in Chapter 2?) they bring to the table. They focus on the orange, they demand the orange, and life will not be worth living unless they get the orange. They have named one possible option for resolving this conflict, elevated it to the best solution in their mind, and made it their demand. When in fact, their "orange" is simply one option.

The "orange" does something for them. It fixes something in their life. It makes something better. Your job, as a need explorer is to figure that out. The only clue you have to what their need really is, in the demand they are making, is their "orange." So let's explore their "orange" to see what future it provides them.

> The "orange" does something for them. It fixes something in their life.

Now that you know the future behavior of the arguing kids (this is a hint pointing to resolution skills we will get into when we learn about conflict's timeline in Chapter 5), let's rewind the tape and go back to the beginning.

Two kids, one orange; what should Karen do?

Ask a question. The number one characteristic of a good need explorer is to ask a ton of questions. Here are three questions that will help in your practice as a need explorer. But first let's look at the one question that never works.

That one question is: "What do you need?"

Does it not make sense, if "knowing their need gets you closer to a resolution", then simply asking "what do you need" is the perfect question? In my experience, it never works. The reason it never works, is they do not know what their need is. The reason they do not know their own need is...here it is....they are lousy need explorers.

Let's try asking Sam and Amy what they need.

Karen: "Sweetheart, what do you need?"

Here is the answer you will get, every time, from every child stuck in a conflict:

Children: "The Orange."

One major reason people get stuck in conflict is they do not know what need they are fighting to meet. The number one reason communication skills do not resolve conflict is they will not get you to their needs. <u>Need exploration is a resolution skill</u>. It is hard to do. It will take a great deal of practice (and failure) on your part to learn it. This skill is not modeled anywhere for you, not at home, at work, at school. You will not see it modeled for you on TV, by actors, by athletes, on commercials, in a sit-com, etc.

Some people find it helpful to distinguish between what the arguing children "want" and their "need." If this is helpful to you, start here.

> Karen: "No honey, the orange is what you want. You would like very much to have that orange, but you do not need that orange. A need is something that satisfies a basic human hunger deep inside all of us. Meeting your need will help you thrive as a human being. So, rather than tell me what you want, tell me what you need."
>
> Sam: "Huh?!"

The distinction works better if you keep it in your head, using it to guide your exploration skills. While in many ways it is a useless practical distinction, because it tends to minimize their stated expectations and outcomes, it can help the explorer practice their skill.

Let's look at a scenario where understanding needs can have life-changing results.

Ken and Karen argued terribly when he first returned from his overseas duty. They even considered divorce. In a private meeting with Karen, her counselor asked her,

"If you could have anything you wanted here today, what would you ask for?"

> Karen: "I would want a divorce decree this minute!"
>
> Counselor: "How would that help you here today?"
>
> Karen: "Every time he got on his high horse, I would have a way to stop him!"
>
> Counselor: "Ok. But how would having a way to stop him, help you?"
>
> Karen: "I still love Ken, but he is always picking on me. He wouldn't be able to pick at me about every little thing. I wouldn't need to defend everything I have done while he was gone."
>
> Counselor: "So, let's say you had a document that gave you all of the power to stop him. How would THAT help you? What would that power give you?"
>
> Karen: "It would give me peace of mind."
>
> Counselor: "So if we could find a way here today to get you peace of mind, a lasting consistent peace of mind without filing for divorce, you would be happy?"
>
> Karen: "Yes, I just don't want to fight anymore."

Notice how hard it was for her to talk about her need. She did not know how to get there. The counselor had to ask enough questions, in many different ways in order to discover her need. We still need to know what "peace of mind" looks like to her. We know a divorce decree is one option that could begin to do that, but now we know her need. It is helpful to know that love is still there. Need Exploration is a hard skill to learn, made harder by the fact that the people you are exploring with cannot effectively help you.

> Ask many questions in different ways to discover the need.

Later, the counselor did need exploration with Ken. His attorney was adamant about applying aggressive tactics in order to bend Karen's will to agree to their demands.

> Attorney: *"We are going to crush her in court. We are going to drag out evidence of her various failings with the children and her irresponsibility with their family finances."*

> Counselor to Ken: *"What do you want here today?"*

> Ken: *"I want her to have to repay the credit cards and for the new car she bought while I was overseas! She has a better job and is making more money than me and doesn't mind saying so."*

Attorney: "And if she doesn't agree with our demands, then she will have to pay even more money as we drag this out in court."

Counselor to Ken: "If you could have anything...If you knew that whatever you asked for this morning, it would be granted to you, no questions asked, what would you ask for?"

Ken: "I just want the bills paid and for all of the arguing to stop. I still care about Karen, but I can't stand the way things are between us."

Counselor to Ken and attorney: "And if this gets dragged out through court, would it mean the bills would still be in your life during all this time and that the arguing would continue?"

Counselor to Ken: "So if we could get the bills paid and the arguing stopped, would you be happy with a resolution that did that for you?"

Ken: "Yes."

Ken's need was getting the bills paid and the arguing stopped, not to punish Karen. By getting his need on the table it could now inform every decision he made. It also gave him focus to make decisions that helped him. He was able to distinguish between those decisions that helped him and the tactics being used by his attorney. By focusing on his need, it was possible to defuse the value of the attorney's aggressive tactics and empower him to make decisions in his own best interest.

Notice the number of questions asked. Notice the future direction many of those questions took. To resolve this conflict, the counselor needed to know the future, so it was necessary to create questions that painted as vivid a picture of the future as possible.

— Three Questions to Get You Started —

Here are some questions to use in need exploration. First, ask the participants to tell you what they want. This will get their demand on the table. They will state their single solution here; they will present their "orange." In the examples above you could ask this question as, "If you could have anything you want, the best of all possible worlds, what would you ask for?"

> **The first question is designed to get their demand out in the open.**

So the first question is designed to get their demand out in the open. You have learned that what they say, more often than not, will not be their need, so don't be fooled. It may be their best of all possible worlds but, in this situation, it is still simply their "orange". Remember, people do not know how to do need exploration on themselves.

Once you have their "orange" on the table, you must explore some characteristics of this "orange" to try and

> Stay focused! Don't be distracted by the answers you are given.

determine what it will do for them. So the second question to ask is, "Why do you want "the orange?"

There are two types of "why" questions: One "why" question wants to know the reasons behind something; the other "why" question wants to know the purpose for something. The need explorer is asking, "for what purpose are you demanding this orange." Inevitably, your person in conflict will answer by giving you the reasons they deserve the "orange."

In the examples above, the counselor tried to get to this by asking, "how will this help you?" Notice how poor Karen was at need exploration. She kept talking about how it would affect Ken's behavior, not how it would help her. The more someone focuses on the other person (remember the person is the problem?), the further away they are getting from knowing their own need. A need explorer's job is to stay focused, do not get distracted by the answers they give you. Had the counselor explored any of the answers she gave, they would have taken him far a-field from what he was looking for. Therefore, one of the skills a need explorer must develop is what NOT to listen to. The danger with listening skills alone is the tangential tracks taken by listening to bad answers given by people who do not know how to explore their own need.

You can take the "for what purpose" question deeper by asking an impact question. "What impact will it have, if you do not get this "orange"? Amy tells me, "I will starve to death!" Sam tells me, "I will fail my science project." Both answers paint a picture of a future event. You are closer to their needs.

> Discover the need and several options become apparent.

You can ask this same question, but from the opposite point of view. Instead of asking, "What impact will it have, if you DO NOT get this "orange"? You can ask, "What impact will it have, if you DO get this "orange"? Often, in asking both questions you get a nuance in their answer that will get you even closer to discovering their need.

Once you have someone's need you can play around with it, trying to get a clearer picture of their future. With the need will come multiple options. Sifting through several options will also create clarity for both the need explorer and the other person.

It is not unusual for someone to experience surprise in the moment of need discovery. Often at the end of a need exploration exercise the person I am working with will have a kind of epiphany. It is as though a light goes on. Knowing their need empowers them. It takes their focus off the other person as the problem and gets them focused on the only thing they can control: their own attitude and their own actions.

I was working with another couple who were entrenched in their pain and stuck in their single solution mindset. They had been in this position for a long time, seeing no way out of the situation. Their prolonged fighting had begun to spill over onto their friends and family creating a widening circle of pain for everyone pulled into their fight. It was then that I was called in.

> When a person discovers their own need, it changes the way they negotiate.

Exploring needs, I discovered one person was leaving the relationship in order to stay healthy. The relationship was hurting their mental and emotional health and they were leaving the relationship in order to regain their health. If health was the need and not moving on would hurt their health, then the question was, "How important are your demands if they cost you your health?" "Are the demands that are keeping you two stuck together, trapped in this unending cycle of disagreement, worth the continued harm to your health?" "If you could end this today, would your journey to health begin?"

Discovering need empowers decision making. A couple of sessions later, the husband came to our session with clarity. "I want to begin my journey of health." He wanted health (his need) more than he wanted his "orange" (his single solution).

Discovery of needs will change the way you negotiate. It changes the way you fight. Discovering needs will change the dynamics of the conflict. Need exploration skills can take you across the threshold of the door your communication skills kept open. By discovering their needs, Ken and Karen now stood squarely in the room of resolution.

— Summary —

In Chapter 2, you were introduced to three dynamics associated with conflict communication: the person becomes the problem, a single solution mindset, and an imbalanced personal state. In the last chapter we looked at five communication techniques for facilitating a healthy venting process and getting one back into a balanced personal state.

Need exploration will get you around the other two conflict communication dynamics. By exploring a person's need, you take their focus off of the other person as the problem and get them talking about themselves. Discovering a person's need will take them out of a single solution mindset. There are many options available for meeting a need, not just the one they have made into their demand, not just the "orange".

Three questions will get you started as a need explorer.

1) What do you want?

2) Why do you want this?

3) What impact will it have on your life if you get this (or don't get this)?

Remember, we all have basic human needs, as Maslow states in his hierarchy of needs. Many of the needs that drive us into a conflict reflect some kind of threat to our basic human needs. Listen for these things when you explore. Try and drive the questioning deeper and deeper. Don't just settle for the first answer they present to you. It is more than likely they will not be able to tell you what their needs are because they don't know how to apply this skill to themselves.

Practice on yourself. After all you are human; you have basic needs. Practice looking deep within yourself and asking what it is you want. Why do you want this? How will it help you? What will it do for you? And follow up with: What will be the impact on your life if you do not get what you are asking for or demanding? As you get better applying this skill to yourself, your skill as a resolver of conflict will improve.

Chapter Four
Need Exploration Exercise

Directions: Explore Ken's need using the skills identified in this chapter. Be careful to distinguish his "needs" from his "want." By identifying his need, the opportunity for good conflict communication is available to Ken and Karen. They may find a resolution without doing damage to their relationship by arguing about everything <u>but</u> the real problem. With the need identified, they have the ability to not make the other person the problem, and focus on real resolution for action that is future oriented.

Remember: Be careful not to solve a need that doesn't exist!

You need to ask:

1. What do you want?

2. Why do you want it?

3. What impact will it have if you do get it, and/or, what impact will it have if you don't get it?

Hint: There is always more than one way to meet a need.

Spending Too Much Money *(Scenario)*

Ken: Lately I've been noticing that you are not able to handle our money. You are spending way too much everywhere you go.

Karen: It's not that I can't handle the money – everything has gone up, the kids are older and eat more, and you are always asking me to get something extra at the grocery store. I do buy when things are on sale and I use coupons.

Ken: Buying on sale and using coupons doesn't make us money. So what happens when we can't afford to keep the lights on or buy gas for the car? I'm the only one working here. You know that we only have one income, and it almost isn't enough to pay for what we need, much less what we want.

1) What do you want? List as many options as you can think of:

   a.

   b.

   c.

   d.

   e.

   f.

2) Why do you want it? List as many options as you can think of:

   a.

b.

c.

d.

e.

f.

3) What impact will it have if you do get it (*your need met*)? List as many options as you can think of:

a.

b.

c.

d.

e.

f.

4) What impact will it have if do not get it (*your need met*)? (List as many options as you can think of:

a.

b.

c.

d.

e.

f.

(A list of options that have been generated for this exercise are located in Appendix A at the back of the book and are also available on our website www.conflictresolutionacademy.com.)

Personal Notes and Lessons Learned

CHAPTER FIVE
The Time to Fight

Conflict follows a timeline. There is a past, a present, and a future. Only two of these can be negotiated. Do you know which two? Almost everyone gets this question wrong. People tend to assume: present and future, because the past can't be changed. But this answer is wrong.

Everyone in conflict negotiates the past. "You didn't do what you said you would." "You did something you were not supposed to do." Often you will hear two people negotiating the past with, "All I said was...." "Well it sounded to me like you were...." Listen when people are fighting. Better yet, listen when you are fighting. Count the number of past tense verbs in your statements.

The assumption is that, if I can get you to agree with me about what "really" happened our argument will be over.

— Negotiating the Past —

Here is a typical conflict scenario:

Karen to Ken: "You didn't take out the garbage <u>again</u> like you said you would."

From here we can get into the skills necessary for getting to resolution of this argument. You might take issue with the quick movement away from the past.

Ken to me: "Wait a minute. My wife thinks I screwed up and is upset with me. If I can explain what happened, then, she would understand and not be upset with me anymore." He wants to create a narrative that sets his actions in a context that will not be "upset worthy." She will forgive him and all will be well with the world once again.

Keep in mind, his narrative was not a lie. He was not trying to make something up to get out of trouble. No, his narrative of the past is true. It is true from his perspective. His wife has another perspective on the past event. It is important to realize, we, as effective conflict managers, are not looking for truth. In fact, experience has taught that <u>the truth does not resolve conflicts</u>. Convincing her of his point of view, of the "truth,"

> There is a past, a present, and a future. Only two of these can be negotiated.

will not necessarily change her frustration. By focusing on the "truth" of the situation, he misses the need his wife was trying to express.

Negotiating the past always leads to defensiveness. By negotiating the past Ken feels he must defend his actions, and Karen feels she must defend her interpretation of his actions. The resolution of this conflict does not lie in the past "facts." It lies in the future, which introduces the fourth secret for managing conflict.

Conflict Management Secret #4:
All resolution is future oriented.

Therefore, in any conflict you want to negotiate the future if you wish for a resolution. Only two time elements can be negotiated in any conflict: the past and the future. Negotiating the past always leads to defensiveness, so negotiate the future. That's where the resolution lies.

— Getting Out of the Past and into the Future —

This is the skill most people don't have. There are three questions for navigating through a conflict keeping the future in mind. However, I must warn you now, there is nothing magical about the questions, and the order in which you ask them. For teaching purposes, the introduction of these questions will sound very mechanical and static. They are not, and if you try to apply this in a mechanical, static, linear structure, you will more than likely escalate the conflict and probably close the door of communication.

These questions are woven into a larger dialogue by a skilled conflict resolver who is paying close attention to the nature and dynamics of the conflict. Knowing the questions is not the skill. The skill comes in knowing how conflict works and weaving them into the conflict appropriately enough to achieve the goal of resolution.

Looking at the "you didn't take out the garbage <u>again</u>" scenario, the first question you want to ask to get to the future is about the past, "What happened?"

The exact words are not important here. What you want to know is what happened to cause her to feel the way she does. Something about you not taking out the garbage caused her to be upset. What was it?

Are you confused? I said negotiating the past would lead to defensiveness, not resolution. So why am I telling you to explore the past? Two reasons: 1) the hurt person needs to talk about what happened to them (venting), and 2) you are looking for a baseline for her emotional response.

> Explore the past, but do not attempt to negotiate it.

What is being asked of you is not to negotiate the past. Some read from this that the past is irrelevant, useless to the resolution process and should be ignored. This is a mistake and discounts the emotional dynamics of conflict. You need to <u>explore</u> the past, <u>not negotiate</u> it. You can explore it without having to defend your version of it. If Ken begins to defend, to correct, to offer an alternative narrative, then he has slipped into negotiating the past.

Exploring the past means Ken is asking questions about how Karen understands the circumstance. Understanding her perspective on the situation gives him the baseline he needs to move forward. If he is going the change the relational damage between the two of them, then he needs to understand how she came to feel the way she does. The resolution is directly related to changing how she feels.

This is why seeking to eliminate emotions, is a disastrous suggestion. Why? By ignoring emotions in conflict we tend to handle conflict poorly. If a proposed solution does not affect her negative feelings then it is not a good resolution to this conflict. That means that one of the tests of a good resolution to any conflict is its impact on the way someone is feeling toward you and/or the situation. But we are getting ahead to the third question when we haven't even introduced the second and most important question.

— The 2nd Question:
The Most Important of the Three —

The second question is the pivot point between the past and the future. This is the question you have in the back of your mind from the very first moment the conflict begins. "What are you asking me to do?"

"What are you asking me to do?" is a future oriented question. As soon as the other person answers this question you are negotiating the future. But here is what will not work.

You might try to shorten the conflict dynamic by asking the future question first. Here is what can happen when you do not pay attention to how conflict works. When you go for the pivot first, wanting to get over the past and get to the issue, the other person can not answer the question. After, blundering through this several times, you will begin to notice a pattern. They need to get the past off of their chest before they can accept any invitation into the future.

> People who have been hurt want their pain to be acknowledged.

As is true of Ken and Karen's argument, what you can conclude from this is: people who are hurt, frustrated by the other's actions, want them to understand first that they have caused them pain. They want them to know, to understand, and in most cases, admit, that they did something wrong and what was done to hurt them.

You should not "cut to the chase," when resolving conflict. But you are welcome to try. If your experience is anything like mine, then what you will find is, even if you ask the second question first, they will answer the first question. Let me illustrate:

> Karen: *"You did not take out the garbage last night, like you promised. You always forget, and you always promise to remember it the next time. You are not dependable."*
>
> Ken: *"What is it you are asking me to do?"*
>
> Karen: *"I shouldn't have to ask you to do anything. You should take responsibility for the things you say you are going to do. I can't even trust your word when you promise to do something. Obviously, just because you promise something does not mean you will keep your word. You forgot to take out the garbage again! Even your promise is worthless."*

Notice she did not answer the future question. This means she is still in phase one of the conflict timeline: the past. You, as a good conflict manager, must join her there if you hope to move forward. It is here, where your communication skills (Chapter Three) should be applied to keep the door of communication open. It is in this phase of the conflict where communication skills are the most valuable.

Do not force the future. Karen needs to vent, she needs to get this off her chest. The conflict cannot move to the future or to the resolution phase, until she is able to do this. This is why it is important to explore the past without negotiating it, because she needs to talk about what you "did" to her.

Stay in the past as an explorer for as long as necessary. Periodically test the waters with a future oriented question. Eventually, she will answer question two for you and negotiating the future begins.

> *Karen: "You did not take out the garbage last night, like you promised. You always forget, and you always promise to remember it the next time. You are not dependable."*
>
> *Ken: "What is it you are asking me to do?"*
>
> *Karen: "I want you to do the dishes! I had to take out the garbage, what you were supposed to do, so now I want you to do the dishes!"*

— Negotiating the Future —

Notice we have a proposal for a future action. This action is offered as a recompense for the failed past action. We are now going to negotiate what the future will look like. Will it look like Ken washing the dishes? Or will it look like Ken not washing the dishes, watching the game instead?"

If Ken says "OK" here, and agrees to wash the dishes, he will fail as a good conflict manager and will be making a huge mistake. This mistake is born mainly out of conflict avoidance.

Most people will make the mistake of going for the "OK" here. "If doing the dishes is what it will take to repair the relationship, then I will do it." But that is not what it will take to repair the relationship. What is required here is not an "OK", but a conflict manager who can do need exploration. It is phase two of the conflict where your need exploration skills (Chapter Four) best apply.

How do you know whether or not her request for washing the dishes is simply a punishment? If it is a punishment for not taking out the garbage, then two things will happen if you agree: 1) you will be agreeing to being punished, and 2) her feelings about the situation will not be affected.

Ken should never agree to punishment. Ken should agree to meet her need. Agreeing to her punishment will not change the emotional baseline. In fact, it will reinforce the emotional baseline. Obviously, her assessment and her feelings of distrust must be right, if Ken agrees to the punishment.

Doing the dishes is her "orange." What will the orange fix for her? He must explore what she wants, why she wants it, and what impact it will have on her life if she does not get the dishes washed.

One of the impacts you need to consider in your need exploration is whether or not it will change the way a person is feeling about you and the situation. One of the tests as to whether or not her proposal is, in fact, a punishment or a need, is its impact on their feelings. If it is a punishment, then their feeling of satisfaction will be short lived; they will not really feel as though this issue has been resolved. And accepting a punishment as a resolution gives them permission to continue punishing you over this issue.

> Never agree to punishment. Instead, agree to meet the need.

You must get to the need if you hope to resolve this. The typical course of this conflict goes to feeling over-worked and under appreciated. The demand to do the dishes is an effort to enforce a reduction or redistribution of the workload (a workload that was unfairly distributed by you forgetting to take out the garbage again, leaving it for her to do, again!).

If the problem is an over-demanding workload, then the need is to find a way to lessen the workload. Remember, there is always more than one way to meet a need (Conflict Management Secret #3). How many different resolution possibilities can you think of that would lessen, lighten, or even completely remove her workload? In my experience, people can think of many.

Imagine if after need exploration and negotiating what the future might look like if Ken offers to do all of the house work for the evening. Suppose he proposes that Karen goes out with her girlfriends and he will take care of the kids and laundry tonight. Do you suppose, if he had indeed applied his need exploration skills effectively, she would reject such a proposal?

What if the proposal went so far as to even negotiate that Ken would do everything tonight, but not do the dishes? Do you think she would accept such an offer?

Most people sense danger here and say, "No", she would not accept the no dishes offer. In fact, fear suggests that she would counter propose: the kids, the laundry, the dishes, her freedom tonight, and for the rest of the week. And, we are back to punishment.

— The Third Question: Benefit —

This happens because most people fail to ask the third question: the benefit question. "How will doing this benefit you, as well as benefit me?"

The benefit question safeguards against punishment.

> Ken: "How will me doing all of the chores and you going out with your girlfriends for a week benefit you?"

> Karen: "It's the least you should do for putting

me in this position again."

Ken: "I understand, I upset you and I am sorry for that, but how would me doing these things benefit you?"

Karen: "I would get a week off from the chores and get some free time."

Ken: "How would getting a week off from the chores and some free time benefit you? And how would doing these things benefit me?"

There are five components of a commitment: well planned, operational, bilateral, realistic, and having positive and negative consequences.[1] If you are going to make a commitment to a future action plan, then consider at least the bilateral nature of commitment. If I do what you are asking, then what are you willing to do in exchange for my doing what you ask? What benefit is there for me in doing what you are asking me to do?

I am not saying I am unwilling to do what you are asking. I just want to ensure that doing what you ask will accomplish my desired outcome. In other words, why would I do all of the chores for a week, giving you a night out every night next week only for you to remain angry with me about the garbage? This is one of the reasons finding the baseline was so important. The baseline tells

1   Fisher, R.,Ury, W., & Patton, B. (1991). *"Getting to Yes: Negotiating agreement without giving in"* (2nd ed.) New York: Penguin

me what happened and why she is upset. This is what I am willing to put effort into changing. I want my future action to affect her feelings in a positive way. Doing them with no assurance of affective change is a mistake and promotes punishment.

> *Ken: "How will me doing all of the chores and you going out with your girlfriends for a week benefit you?"*

> *Karen: "It's the least you should do for putting me in this position again."*

> *Ken: "I understand, I upset you and I am sorry for that, but how would me doing these things benefit you?"*

> *Karen: "I would get a week off from the chores and get some free time."*

> *Ken: "How would doing these things benefit me?"*

> *Karen: "You would see what it is like to have to do all the work around here and appreciate how hard it is."*

> *Ken: "OK. I am willing to consider doing what you are asking me to do, but if I do, will you, then, no longer be mad with me about the garbage?"*

Usually, the benefit question goes something like this: "I will be willing to see that the chores are done and you can take the rest of the night off to relax. I am sorry for the problems my irresponsibility has caused you, and I don't want you to stay mad at me. If you get the night off, would you forgive me for the garbage?"

The point was not the garbage. The garbage was a symptom of a larger problem. The problem was Karen's feeling stuck with all the work around the house and Ken being oblivious to what it takes to keep up with it all. She wants him to get it. She wants him to understand and appreciate all that she does. She wants Ken to get off his lazy heinie and pitch in. It's not about the garbage; it's not about the dishes; it's about him getting it. Besides, a night off would help her and maybe indicate that Ken understands a little about what Karen has to do every night. If he can't get there, they will not resolve this conflict.

Most people completely fail doing the benefit phase. Ken might agree to do the dishes, thinking he is making a (bilateral) commitment, only to find out that doing what Karen asked did nothing to change her mood, feelings, or attitude toward him. The result is twofold: Ken resents having agreed and resents doing it. "Why do I even try? I did what you asked, and I still have to sleep on the couch?" And Karen stays unsatisfied and angry because she got what she asked for instead of what she needed.

> The garbage is not the point. It is just a symptom of the problem.

The next time you argue, you will be less likely to agree to anything she asks you to do, remembering that last time it got you nowhere. "I can never satisfy you. Nothing can make you happy!" You become distant and she becomes a "nag." This happens not because you are bad at relationships, not because you are incompatible, not because you are growing apart, but because you do not understand how conflict works.

Either one could have "won" this argument and not have had to do anything at all, but at what cost? "Winning" is not always a win. By meeting a need, there is the option for both parties to come out winning, and as an added bonus, without any damage to the relationship that might sabotage future negotiations.

— Summary —

Phase one of a conflict corresponds to the past. Explore the past, do not negotiate the past. Use communication skills to explore the other person's understanding of what happened. The phase one question to typically ask is:

> "What happened that caused you to be so upset?"

Phase two of a conflict corresponds to the future. The future is where resolution lies, not in the past. Use your resolution skills to explore the needs of the other person, keeping your needs in mind as well. The phase two question to ask is:

"What is it you are asking me to do?"

Phase three of a conflict corresponds to your commitment to a particular future. You want to commit to an action plan that will positively affect the emotional response created by the other person's perspective on your past action. That is, you want to commit to something that will produce an outcome that at least will not endanger your needs and at best meet both of our needs. The phase three question to ask is:

"What benefits will come from doing what is being asked of me?"

There are two aspects to negotiating the future. The first is raising the pivot point question that gets us out of the past, into proposals for future action, and applying need exploration skills. The second aspect is understanding the mutual benefits of any proposed future action plan for both parties, and applying your negotiation skills.

There are three skills necessary for a great conflict resolver to master: communication skills, resolution skills, and negotiation skills. Communication skills correspond to exploring the past and healthy venting, keeping the door of communication open. Remember, you cannot resolve a conflict with someone you are not talking to. Then, resolution and negotiation skills correspond to negotiating the future. Resolution skills get you across the threshold of the door your communication skills kept open, and negotiation skills navigate you to an action plan that produces bilateral benefits.

Remember, all this sounds pretty mechanical here. There is nothing magical about these three phase questions. Learning these questions is the easy part. Listening for the three phases of a conflict is not that hard. Knowing when to ask what question, weaving your skills into the conversation in such a way that understands conflict dynamics is more difficult.

These skills take time to incorporate into daily living and allow you to change the way you think about conflict. It is not the bad, evil thing you were taught to avoid at all cost. You must begin to understand that the cost of avoiding conflict is heftier than you were led to believe. You lose so much when you try to live as though it is possible to eliminate conflict from your life. Conflict can be your friend. It can bring you so many positive things, if you will learn how conflict works and utilize a few effective skills to pull out its positive potential.

Practicing these skills has changed many lives. We hope they bring you similar success.

Chapter Five

The Time to Fight Worksheet

1) Think about your last argument (either in a personal setting or in your professional setting).

a. What was your "orange"?

b. To what end were you "demanding" this?

c. What impact would it have had in your life if you <u>did not</u> get this?

d. What impact would it have ad in your life if you <u>did</u> get this?

2) What do you think your need was?

3) List at least ten things that could be done to meet this need. Remember to put on the list your "demand."

a.

b.

c.

d.

e.

f.

g.

h.

i.

j.

4) Think about your last argument (either in a personal setting or in your professional setting).

a. Where were you stuck in the past?

b. What could you have said to explore the past (not negotiate it) Summarizing?

c. What could you have asked to explore the past
    Asking a Probing Question?

d. What could you have said to explore the past
    Validating when you could?

e. What could you have said to explore the past
    Identifying Emotions?

5) Remembering parts of your last argument, list
   any criticisms directed toward you.

a.

b.

c.

6) Translate the Positive Request in each of the criticisms listed in #5.

a.

b.

c.

7) Think about your last argument (either in a personal setting or in your professional setting).

a. What proposal was being asked of you? What was their "orange"?

b. Was their proposal a punishment?

c. If so, write a question (without using the word "punishment") you could ask. Consider a question using the word "benefit" and one not using the word "benefit."

d. Repeat their proposal to yourself and say: "That's one option."

e. To what end were they "demanding" this?

f. What impact would it have had in their life if they <u>did not</u> get this?

g. What impact would it have had in their life if they <u>did</u> get this?

8) What do you think their need was?

9) List at least ten things that could be done to meet this need. Remember to put on the list their "demand" of you.

a.

b.

c.

d.

e.

f.

g.

h.

i.

j.

10) Put a check next to the things you might have considered doing on the list of items under #9.

11) Put a check next to the things you might have considered accepting on the list of items under #3.

Personal Notes and Lessons Learned

Dr. Rick Voyles and Carol Rice may be contacted at:

CONFLICT RESOLUTION ACADEMY, LLC
P. O. BOX 724506
ATLANTA, GA 31139
770-435-5009
E-mail – conflictacademy@aol.com
www.conflictresolutionacademy.com

Appendix A
Need Explorations Options Exercise

***

Poor Money Management
Exploring Ken's Need

Thinking about the exercise you did at the end of Chapter 4, here are some options we created, and an analysis of what some of the responses might be around the discussion of Karen's poor money management.

Remember, there are three major questions to begin your exploration of Ken's need. For this exercise, we assume that Ken has one need, whereas, in a more complicated conflict, you may discover that an individual has more than one need motivating his or her decision making.

We will be using the three questions: What do you want? Why do you want it? What impact will it have on your life if you don't get and if you do get it? (It being what they want.)

I find, and expect, the answers Ken gives first do NOT have enough focus, or quality, to be of much use for exploration of his need. I find this to be true because just about every human being I have worked with is typically unable to identify his or her own need. This is a skill that is not taught, and therefore, not practiced well. You just need to recognize that the first answers you get may be useless in your discovery of Ken's need, but they are helpful in figuring out what he doesn't need.

For the sake of this exercise, I put the resolution skills in Karen's hands:

Question #1: What do you want?

Karen: "Ken, I can see you are upset about our money situation and you are frustrated with me. Can you tell me what you want; what it is you are asking for here?"

Ken: "I want you to stop spending so much money. You are being careless and thoughtless with your spending, and it has got to stop!"

Ken's response is not helpful to Karen, and if she focuses on what he has just said, she will go down a path of unproductive escalation of the argument that will take them both further away from finding a resolution. So, how do we know his response is not helpful? An easy test in this situation is to determine <u>who</u> is the subject of the sentence. If you don't determine who is the subject of the sentence, you might jump to explore the question itself.

Immediately, I can see options like these being thrown out on the table:

Options:

1. Stop spending money.
2. Give Ken the checkbook.
3. Create a budget.
4. Consult Ken about the budget before you spend

money.

5. Ask permission to spend money.

6. Karen can get a job.

7. Karen can ask her family for money.

8. Ken can get a second job so money wouldn't be so tight.

9. Ken can do all of the shopping and handle the money.

10. Ken can give Karen an allowance to spend.

Because Ken is talking about Karen, the subject of his sentence is <u>Karen</u>. This is what Karen can do to stop spending money "foolishly." How does that meet Ken's need – and, is it really Ken's need?

It will be possible to discover Ken's need only when Ken begins talking about himself. Karen asked what Ken wanted. Clearly, he wants Karen to "do something." It is not Ken's *need* that Karen manage their money. If it helps you at all, think of the difference between what Ken *wants* and what Ken *needs*. If you focus on Karen's money management skills, you will miss Ken's need. However, his answer is anticipated and is not useless to the exploration process. The point is to not settle on the answer to the first question as the successful discovery of Ken's need.

Question #2: Why do you want it?

Karen: "I can see how managing our money better could help both of us and that is something I am willing to explore more with you. But I'm curious. Out of all the things you could have asked for, you picked that one. Why that one? Why are you asking that more thought and care be put into my spending habits? "

Ken: *"Because you are going to drive us into bankruptcy if you don't stop all of your frivolous spending."*

For the purpose of this exercise, I am making Ken look really bad. It is as though he has no communication/resolution skills at all. But, exploring the worst case scenario can have educational value. Ken has answered the wrong "why" question. How do I know that?

There are two types of "why" question answers. The first is: defend, to me, why you are asking for that.

Ken has answer Karen with a defense for why he is asking for what he is asking for. If we are going to discover Ken's need, we have to get an answer to the second "why" question.

The second is: for what purpose are you asking for that?

Here is Karen's answer:

Karen: *"Ok. I get that. So can you tell me, how will putting more thought and care into my spending habits help you?"*

Ken: *"I won't have to worry about whether or not we will lose the house."*

121

Ah-ha, we are a step closer to finding out Ken's need. Notice Ken is starting to talk about himself (what he is worried about).

> Karen: "Do your worry a lot about losing the house?"

> Ken: "No, only when you spend all of our money."

Oops, a step backward. However, let's see if Karen can handle this and be able to keep a forward momentum of her exploration.

> Karen: "I didn't know you worried about losing the house, or that this was putting such a strain on you. I can see better how working out a spending plan might help take the stress off of you (and in turn off of our relationship).

See, I told you she was good. There is huge temptation here for the resolver to assume that his need is the house. After all, food, clothing, shelter are human basic needs. But we have not gotten to our third question yet, so don't jump to a conclusion and start assuming that everything is easily worked out.

> Karen: "Wow, I didn't know you were worried about losing the house! If we did lose the house, it would really be awful. Tell me though, what are you thinking it would mean for you if we lost the house? What impact would it have on you?"

> Ken: "I cannot begin to explain to you what

that would be like for me. I think I would die of the embarrassment and the shame. How would I look to the other guys if, suddenly, my family and I are living in a cardboard box? I do not think I could ever face my father again. I am supposed to be the provider for my family. What does it say to others if I can't keep a roof over my family's head? "

Do you hear the basic human need driving Ken's engagement in this conflict?

Karen: "I would never want to be a part or a cause of something like that happening to you. I can see that would be devastating to you."

Now see what happens -

Karen: "What can we do to show everyone what a wonderful and responsible provider you are? "

And so begins option generation (not around her spending habits, but ways to make sure he is not embarrassed in front of his family and friends about his ability to support his own family):

Options:

1. What if we paid off the house?
2. What if the kids never wore hand-me-downs?
3. What if we moved to a gated community?
4. What if we drove a better car?
5. What if .....

These are really different options than the ones generated after the first question was asked! You can see how they are more appropriate to protect his pride and send the message to others that he is successful at taking care of his family.

But notice: What if Karen puts more thought and care into her spending? Is that not an option that would work to meet the need that was stated? Yes.

Then why in the world did we go through all of this effort? We are right back at the beginning. Ken asked for her to spend less and her doing so would, in fact, meet Ken's need. Why not just have Karen do what Ken said he wanted?

Here is why: First, do we know that Karen is, in fact, spending money unwisely? No, we do not.

Could she think that by doing what Ken wants her to do, she would be admitting that she is irresponsible with money? Maybe.

Do we think she would be willing to do what Ken is asking if she thought, for a moment, it meant agreeing with him that she spends money irresponsibly? Who knows?

And last, if there are indeed multiple ways to meet Ken's needs, together, could they find one solution on the list that they generated, that they could both say "Yes" to? I think so.

My experience is that by exploring needs, you exponentially increase the chances of finding a mutually satisfying resolution. A mutually satisfying resolution helps to create an atmosphere of trust and a willingness to work together to meet each other's need in a future situation.

www.conflictresolutionacademy.com

Dr. Richard Voyles, President of Conflict Resolution Academy, located in Smyrna Georgia, has a broad-based knowledge in the area of alternative dispute resolution techniques, mediation and leadership development. He travels internationally training people in the areas of prejudice reduction, cross-cultural communication, conflict management, management and leadership skills. As a Registered Neutral with the State of Georgia, he works with the court systems to mediate disputes for everything from Civil cases to Special Education, Elder Care, Divorce and Couples issues. With a background in peacekeeping and diversity, Dr. Voyles has served on the Board of Directors for the Interfaith Coalition of Atlanta, and as a Commissioner for the Georgia Commission on the Holocaust. He currently serves on the Board of Directors for the Georgia Association for Conflict Resolution. His credits include designing training programs for leadership, diversity and conflict management for both corporate and federal organizations. His most recent projects include Relationship Skills training and Church Conflict program design and implementation. He is a published author and a highly sought after speaker and coach across the United States.

Carol Rice, Owner/Partner of Conflict Resolution Academy, LLC, is a Certified Conflict Manager (CCM), with over 20 years of experience in dealing with conflict management in both the private and public sectors. With a focus on providing interactive skills for dealing with difficult people, Ms. Rice has a strong desire to work with members of the military who are experiencing problems that are unique to Soldiers and their families. As the daughter of a career Army officer and the wife of an Air Force veteran, she understands, firsthand, the impact that being a part of the military family can have on relationships. As an owner/partner in Conflict Resolution Academy in Atlanta, GA, she has made it her goal to empower people to make decisions in their own best interest and to help them resolve their disputes at the lowest level possible. Ms. Rice puts strong emphasis on early intervention and alternate dispute resolution options in her work. She consults with a wide variety of clients dealing with relationship issues in a variety of settings, and has helped them find productive ways to nurture those relationships that are important to them.